I Love Horses

Thoroughbreds

Maria Koran

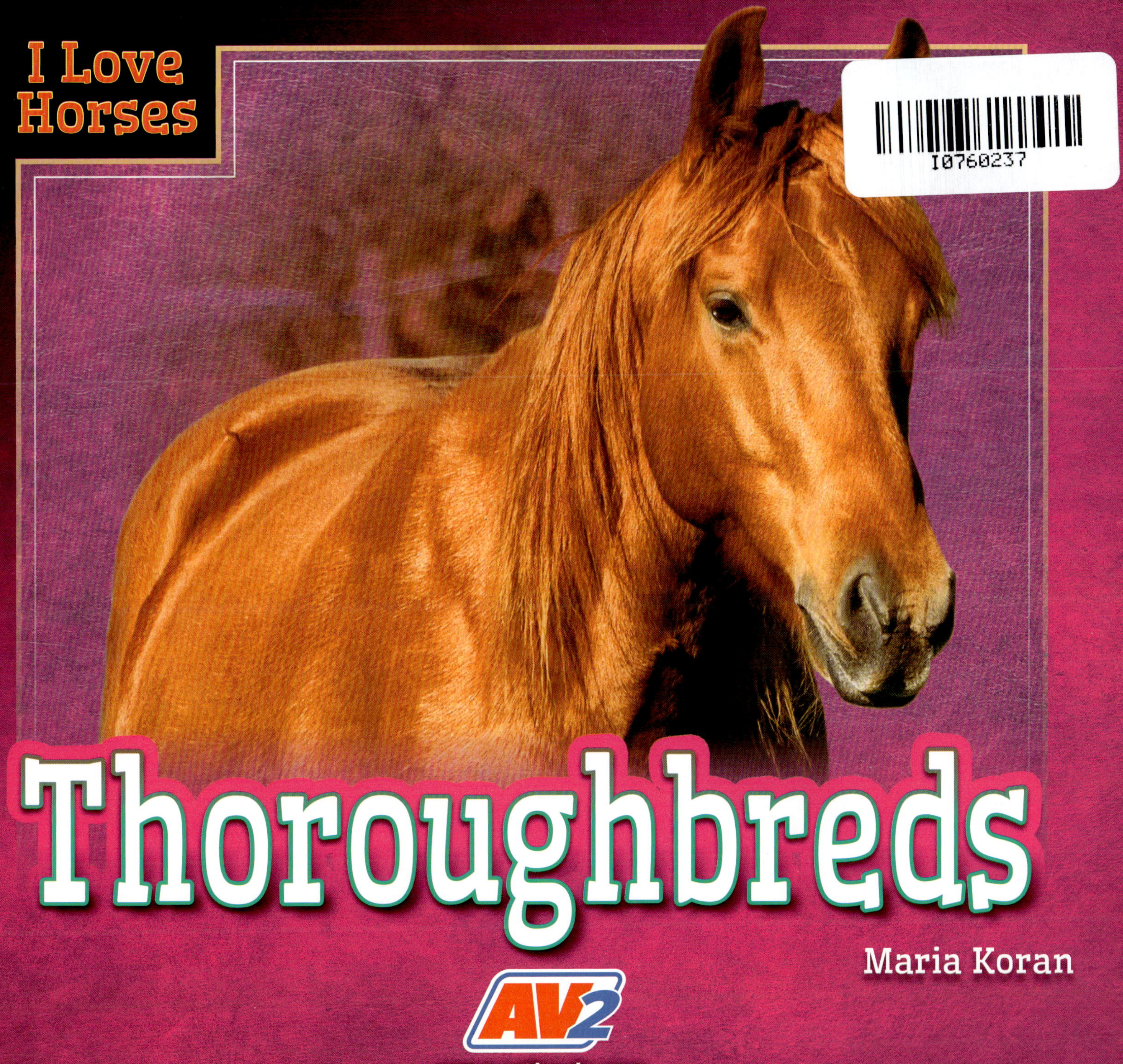

AV2
www.av2books.com

Step 1
Go to **www.av2books.com**

Step 2
Enter this unique code
APCLDO4LF

Step 3
Explore your interactive eBook!

AV2
I Love Horses
Thoroughbreds
Start!

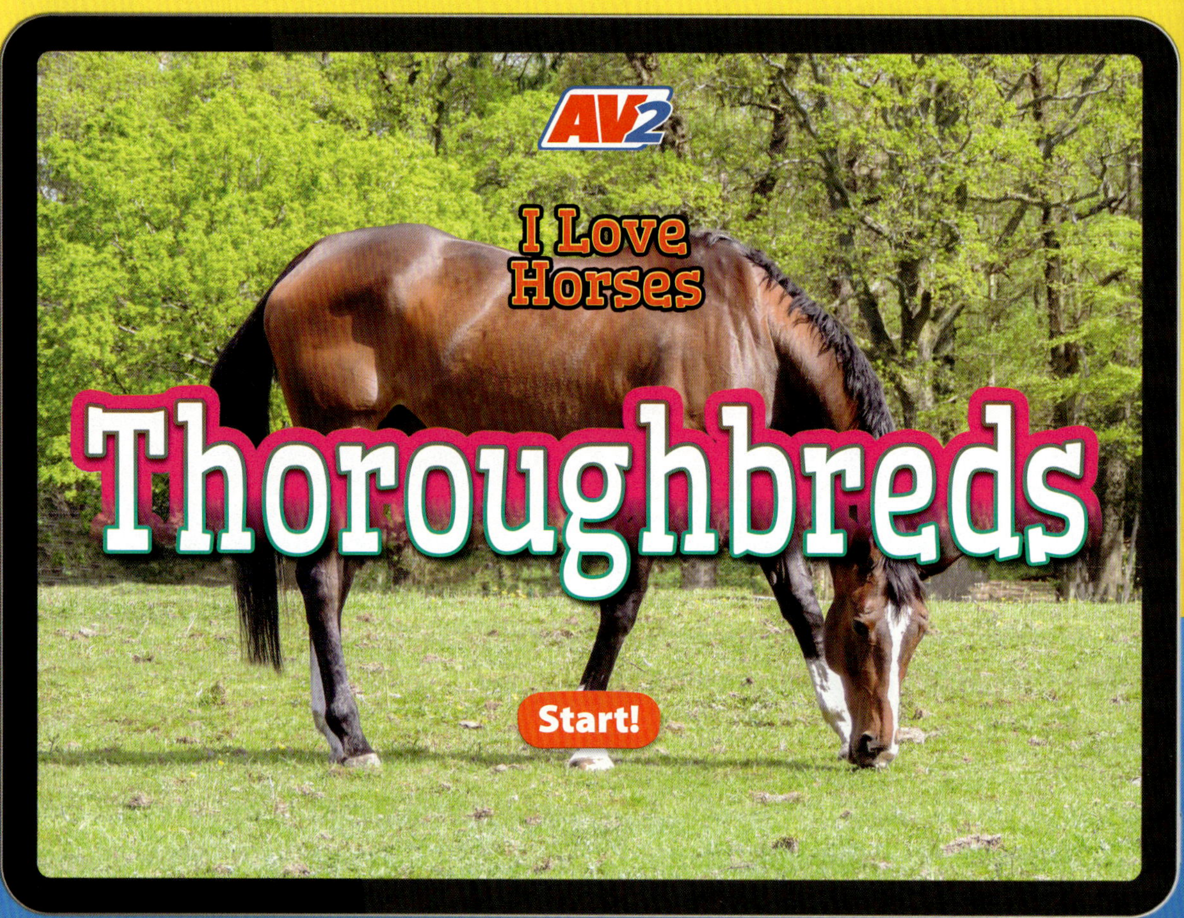

AV2 is optimized for use on any device

Your interactive eBook comes with...

Audio
Listen to the entire book read aloud

Videos
Watch informative video clips

Weblinks
Gain additional information for research

Try This!
Complete activities and hands-on experiments

Key Words
Study vocabulary, and complete a matching word activity

Quizzes
Test your knowledge

Slideshows
View images and captions

Thoroughbreds

CONTENTS

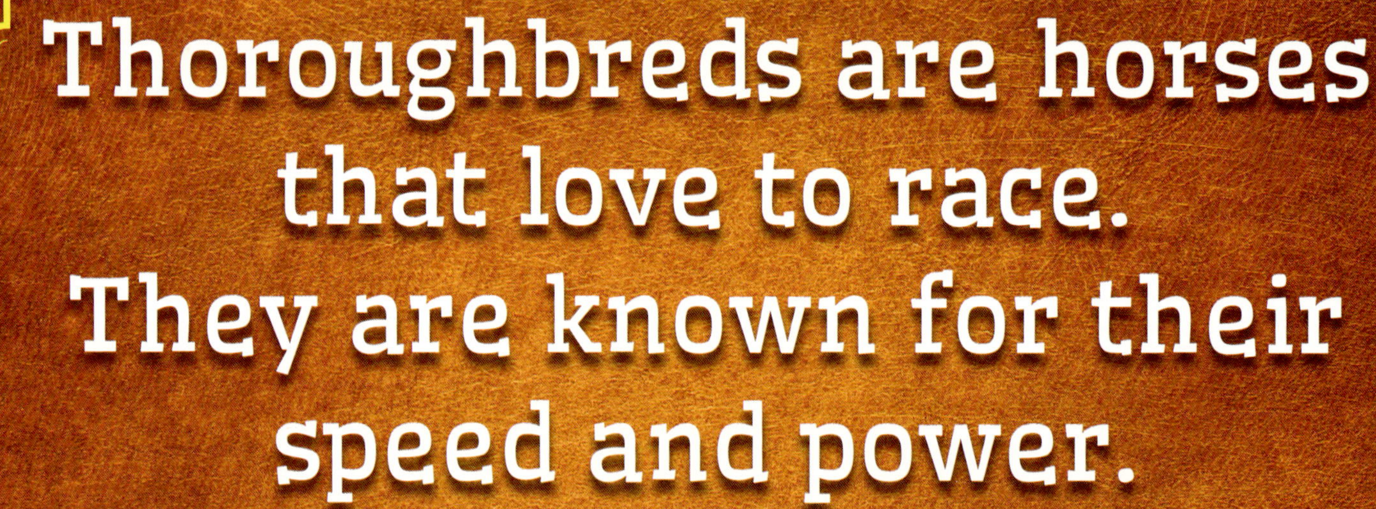

Thoroughbreds are horses that love to race. They are known for their speed and power.

Nearly 40,000 horse races are held in North America each year.

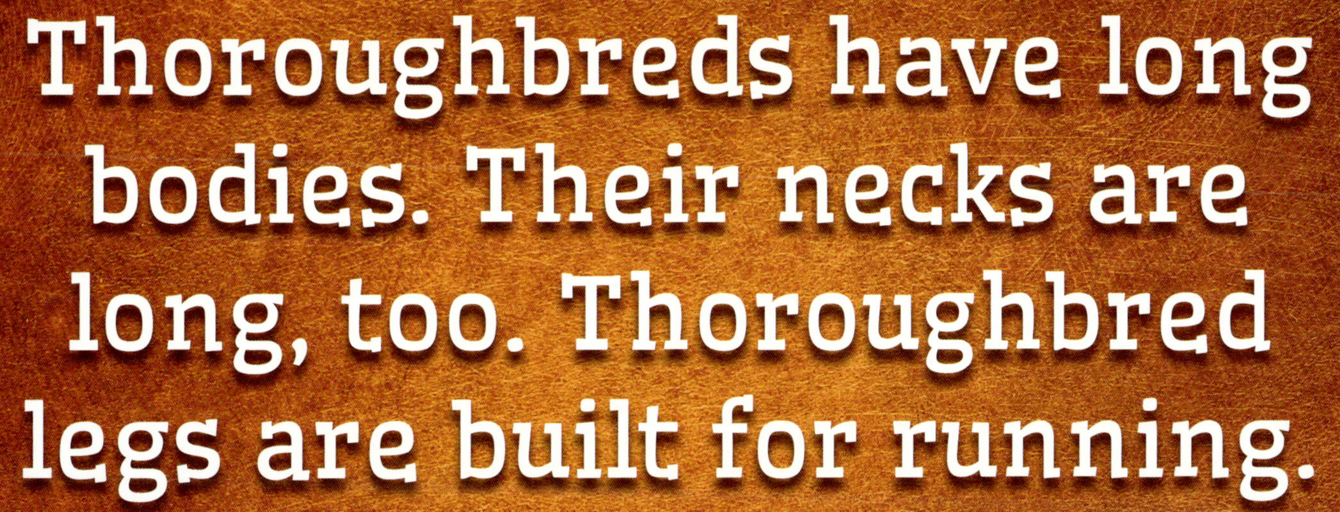

Thoroughbreds have long bodies. Their necks are long, too. Thoroughbred legs are built for running.

Thoroughbreds weigh up to 1,300 pounds (590 kilograms).

Thoroughbreds have one main color. They are often brown or black.

Many Thoroughbreds also have white faces or legs.

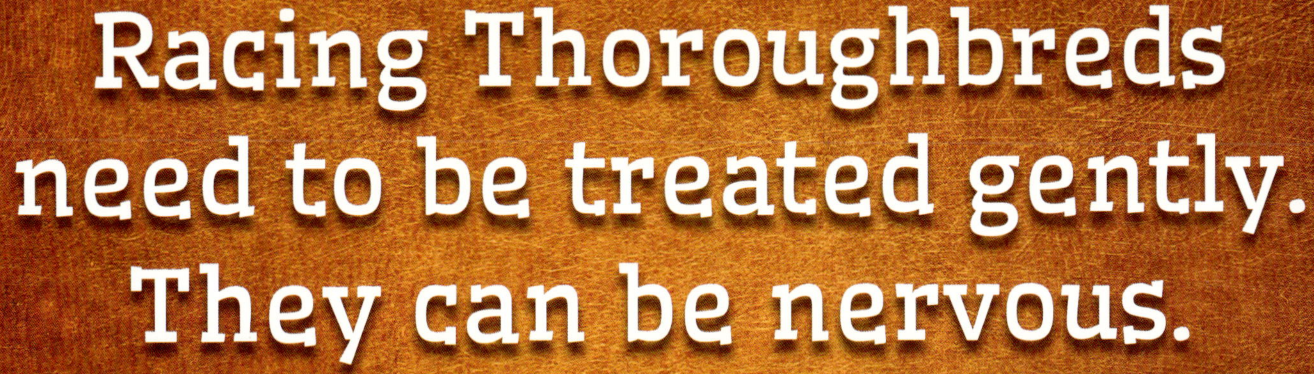

Racing Thoroughbreds need to be treated gently. They can be nervous.

Thoroughbreds that have stopped racing are usually calm.

Many Thoroughbreds run in races. This is a very popular sport.

These horses learn to race when they are young.

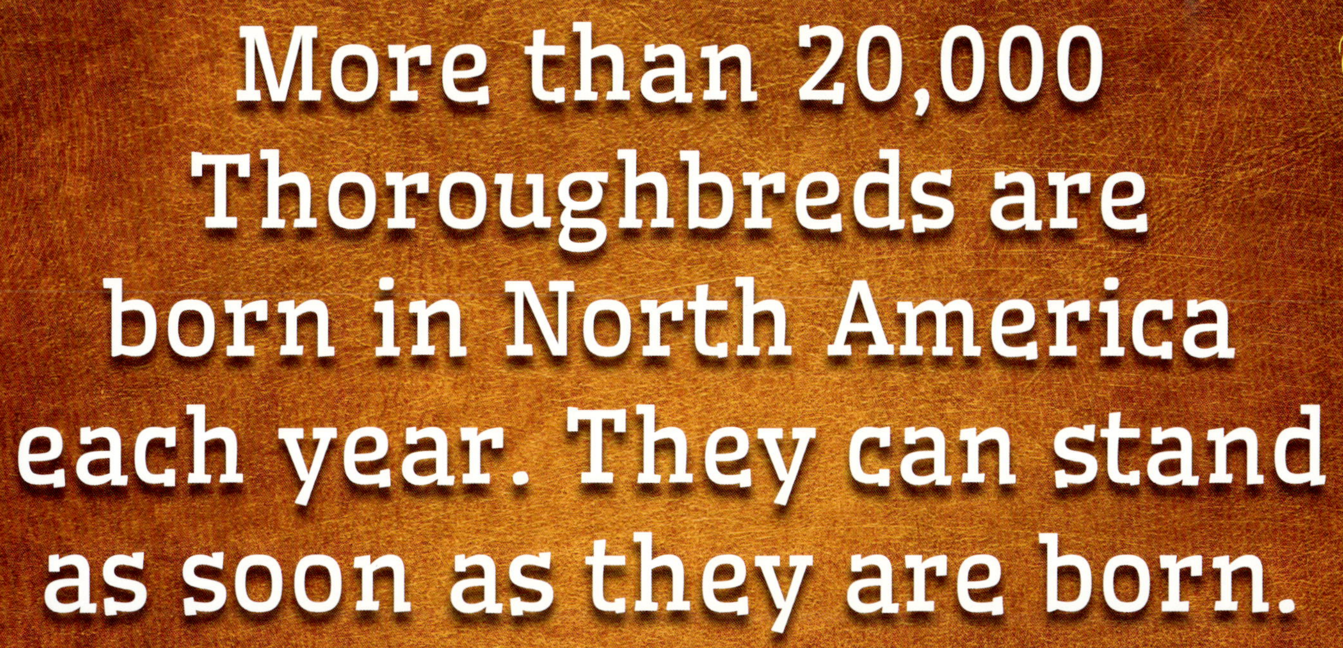

More than 20,000 Thoroughbreds are born in North America each year. They can stand as soon as they are born.

Newborn Thoroughbreds weigh about 110 pounds (50 kg).

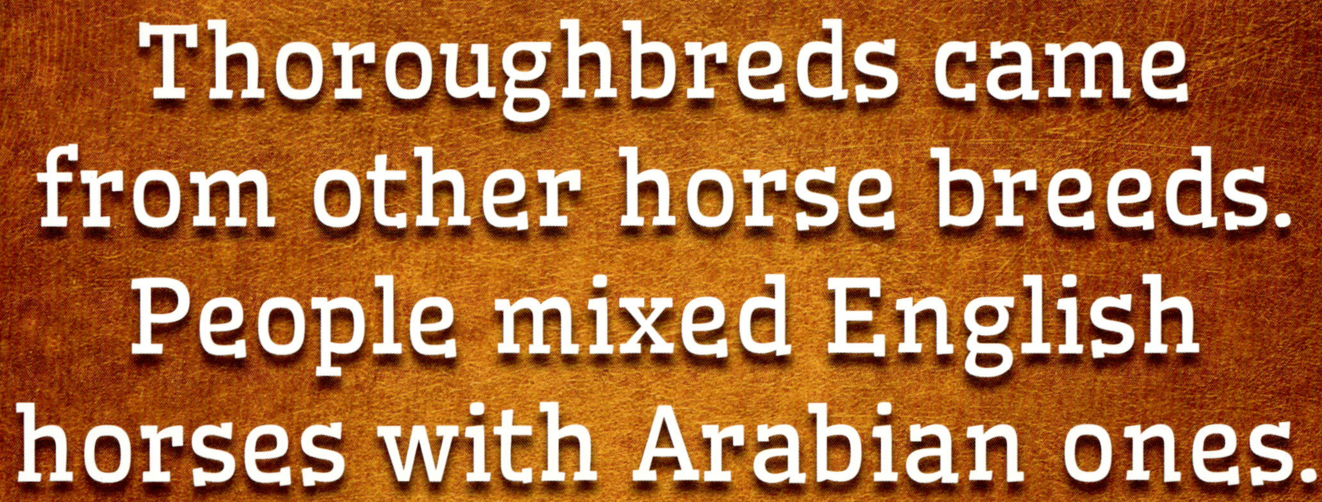

Thoroughbreds came from other horse breeds. People mixed English horses with Arabian ones.

The first Thoroughbreds appeared more than 300 years ago.

Americans saw these fast horses. They wanted to ride them.

They brought Thoroughbreds to North America and held races.

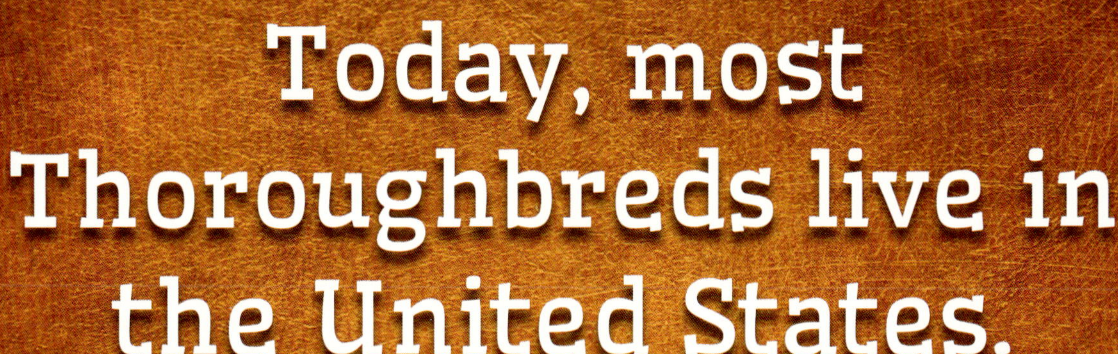

Today, most Thoroughbreds live in the United States.

However, these speedy horses can also be found all over the world.

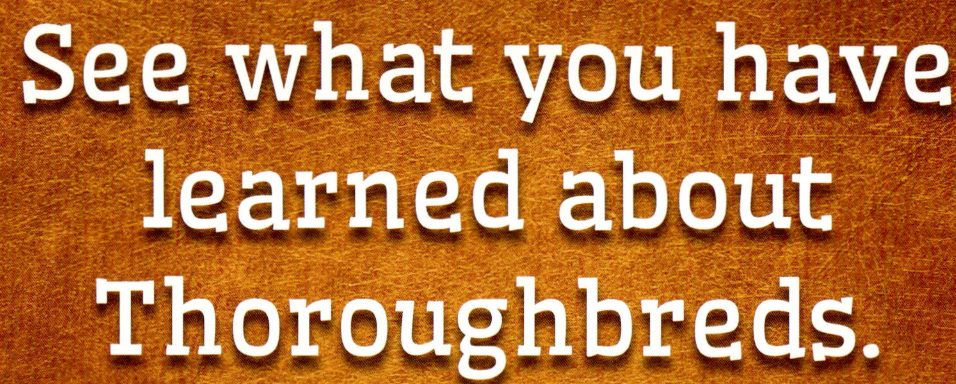

See what you have learned about Thoroughbreds.

Which of these pictures show Thoroughbreds?

KEY WORDS

Research has shown that as much as 65 percent of all written material published in English is made up of 300 words. These 300 words cannot be taught using pictures or learned by sounding them out. They must be recognized by sight. This book contains 54 common sight words to help young readers improve their reading fluency and comprehension. This book also teaches young readers several important content words, such as proper nouns. These words are paired with pictures to aid in learning and improve understanding.

Page	Sight Words First Appearance
4	and, are, each, for, in, known, that, their, they, to, year
7	have, long, too, up
8	also, faces, many, often, one, or, white
11	be, can, need
12	a, is, learn, run, these, this, very, when, young
15	as, more, soon, than
16	came, first, from, other, people, with
18	Americans, saw, them
21	all, found, live, most, over, the, world

Page	Content Words First Appearance
4	horses, North America,power, speed, Thoroughbreds
7	bodies, legs, necks
8	color, markings
11	calm, nervous
12	races, sport
16	breeds
21	United States

Published by AV2
350 5th Avenue, 59th Floor New York, NY 10118
Website: www.av2books.com

Library of Congress Control Number: 2019954943

ISBN 978-1-7911-1971-3 (hardcover)
ISBN 978-1-7911-1972-0 (softcover)
ISBN 978-1-7911-1973-7 (multi-user eBook)
ISBN 978-1-7911-1974-4 (single-user eBook)

Printed in Guangzhou, China
1 2 3 4 5 6 7 8 9 0 24 23 22 21 20

022020
100919

Project Coordinator: John Willis Art Director: Terry Paulhus

AV2 acknowledges Alamy, Getty, iStock, Minden Pictures, and Shutterstock as the primary image suppliers for this title.